MUSIC READING UNLIMITED:
A Comprehensive Method
for High School Choirs

Level I

Student Edition

Vivian C. Munn

B533

TABLE OF CONTENTS

MUSIC READING UNLIMITED:
A Comprehensive Method for High School Choirs

Introduction

This book presents a comprehensive choral method for developing advanced music reading skills. It is ideal for any choir that has mastered the following basic fundamentals of music reading:

- the ability to read in the major keys of C, G, and F
- the ability to read *easy* skips within the tonic, dominant, and subdominant triads
- the ability to read rhythm patterns that incorporate whole notes through eighth notes used in pairs

LEVEL I presents the following concepts:

Rhythmic
- dotted quarter notes, eighth notes and rests
- triplets
- the half note as the beat unit
- compound time
- the eighth note as the beat unit

Tonal
- all major keys
- diatonic interval studies
- supertonic, mediant, and submediant triads
- natural and harmonic minor keys
- modulation to and from major and minor tonality
- the altered tone—"fi" (raised fourth scale degree)

LEVEL II presents the following concepts:

Rhythmic
- sixteenth note patterns
- syncopation
- more difficult compound time studies
- meters of 5 and 7
- changing and combined meters

Tonal
- modulation to the dominant key
- the altered tone—"te" (lowered seventh scale degree)
- modulation to the subdominant key
- harmonic and melodic minor studies
- modulation to and from minor keys
- chromatic scale studies
- chromatic tones and altered chords
- modulation to parallel keys

Music Reading Unlimited, LEVEL I contains eleven units of carefully-graded, sequential musical studies. Each unit in the Instructor's Edition features: 1) an introduction with teaching tips; 2) a clearly stated purpose for each exercise in the unit; and 3) a brief description of the content of each exercise. Most units contain a combination of unison, two-part, and four-part exercises. The unison drills introduce concepts which are then practiced in two-part studies. The two-part exercises are sometimes written in a treble-bass format, but often appear in SATB voicing so that all singers have the opportunity to read their parts within a four-stave context like that of choral music. The SATB studies provide the opportunity for practice and mastery of concepts in four-part harmony.

How to Use This Book

This book is designed to *teach* advanced music reading concepts to the high school choir. The exercises are intended to function as short pedagogical studies which carefully aid in the training of the ear, eye, and mind. The melodies and harmonies are conventional and traditional so that a moderate degree of success can be achieved on the first reading. However, most of the exercises are designed to function as music reading studies, rather than sight-reading drills. Explain, study, and practice them several times (if necessary) for complete understanding and mastery. Once students have mastered the concepts, they are ready to transfer that learning to the actual reading of choral music.

It is extremely important that all exercises are practiced—including the first reading—*without* the aid of the piano. Singers will not develop necessary aural and sight-singing skills if the piano plays their part before or while they are singing it. A piano reduction is provided for the four-part exercises, but it is to be used *only* as an aid to the teacher. Use the keyboard to give the tonic pitch, ask the choir to establish the tonality by singing the major scale and/or outlining the tonic triad, and proceed to read the exercise. Conduct all readings unaccompanied and strive to develop in your singers the ability to "forge ahead" even when they are not sure of the next pitch. Train them to do what instrumentalists do—skip a note or two and come in on the following note or on beat one of the next measure—but always keep going.

LEVEL I is most effective if the units are studied in the order presented. However, since mastery of fundamentals is assumed, the units may be studied out of order to correlate the teaching of concepts with the choir's concert repertoire.

The musical exercises are based on a tonality-centered approach which trains students to perceive and sing melodies within a tonal context. They are equally adaptable to either the "movable do" system of pitch-reading, the traditional "movable number" system, or a "hybrid movable number" system developed by the author. All employ the concept in which "do" or "one" is assigned to the tonic note of a major scale; and they use the "la minor" principle in which "la" or "six" is assigned to the tonic note of its relative minor. Since each system has advantages and disadvantages, the system chosen should be based upon the musical backgrounds and experience of both the students and teacher. However, one of the strongest arguments for choosing the "movable do" system is that students can be taught hand signs to accompany the solfege syllables, and thus reinforce their learning. If your singers use solfege to read, be sure to teach them hand signs, and insist they use them. Most important is that you choose a pitch-reading system and that you use it consistently when teaching reading and when rehearsing. For purposes of illustration and discussion in this book, solfege syllables and numbers are both used.

"Movable do" system

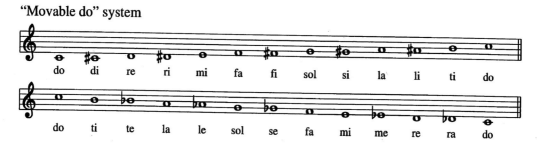

The "hybrid movable number" system uses numbers on all diatonic pitches (with "sev" used on seven). It borrows solfege syllables for the altered pitches. The syllable "ti" is used for all raised scale degrees except four, which is called "fi". Since more than one altered tone rarely occurs in close proximity within an exercise or piece, the use of "ti" for most raised pitches presents few problems. It also aids singers vocally in "sharping" or raising the pitch. In melodic minor ("la minor"), the altered tones are differentiated by the use of "fi" and "ti". The "hybrid movable number" system uses the term "te" for all lowered scale tones.

"Hybrid movable number" system

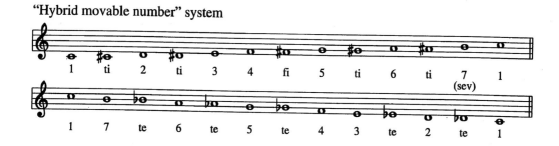

In order to rehearse effectively, it is imperative that high school singers know pitch names and are able to function in both the treble and bass clefs. Take the opportunity throughout the book to ask all singers to read both the treble and bass parts in the two-part exercises.

Just as imperative as a pitch-reading system for singers is a rhythm-reading system. A variety of counting systems are effective; however, for advanced singers, it is strongly recommended that you choose a number counting system in which the beat is assigned an Arabic numeral based upon its position in the measure. Advanced singers (who often have opportunities to sing with instrumentalists) need to learn a number counting system that 1) accounts for the position of beats within a measure, and 2) coordinates the conductor's beat with the specific beat in each measure.

A traditional number counting system is illustrated below:

Key: e = ee   + = and   a = uh

Broken lines under sustained notes indicate fundamental beats which should be pulsated vocally when students are first learning new rhythmic patterns. When introducing new patterns that contain rests, ask singers to whisper the appropriate number or syllable, or sound "sh" for the duration of the rest.

UNIT I

A REVIEW OF BASIC FUNDAMENTALS
$\frac{2}{4}$, $\frac{3}{4}$ and $\frac{4}{4}$ Meters
Whole Notes through Quarter Notes with Corresponding Rests
Eighth Notes in Pairs
Keys of C, F, G, Bb and D Major
Tonic, Subdominant and Dominant Seventh Chords

Exercises 1 – 4   o, ♩., ♩, ♩ and rests

$\frac{4}{4}$, $\frac{3}{4}$, and $\frac{2}{4}$ meters

Physically show the pulse as you read and combine these exercises.

4. A.

B.

C.

D.

Exercises 5 – 11   Tonal Center Singing
Keys of G and C Major

5.

6.

7.

8.

9.

10.

11.

10

20.

21.

14

24. A.

B.

C.

D.

25.

26.

UNIT II

Dotted Quarter Notes
Keys of E♭ and E, and A and A♭ Major
Eighth Notes and Rests

The use of eighth notes and rests involves the rhythmic principle—division of the beat. The arrows in the following example illustrate the division of the beat into downbeats and upbeats.

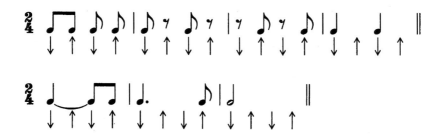

Exercises 1 – 5   Dotted quarter–eighth note Pattern

Think and feel "two downbeats followed by a quick note" when reading dotted quarter notes that occur on the beat.

Counting the rhythm.

Actively demonstrate the downbeat-upbeat principle through toe tapping, hand patting, or arm movements as you read these exercises.

5.

Exercises 6 – 11   Keys of E♭ and E Major

E♭ Major: the key name and tonic pitch are the name of the next to the last flat (E♭)

do	re	mi	fa	sol	la	ti	do
1	2	3	4	5	6	7	1

6.

E Major: the key name and tonic pitch are the note name above the last sharp (D♯)

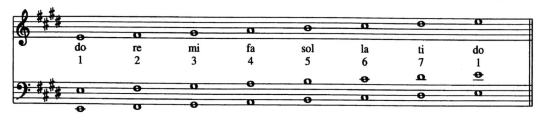

9.

10.

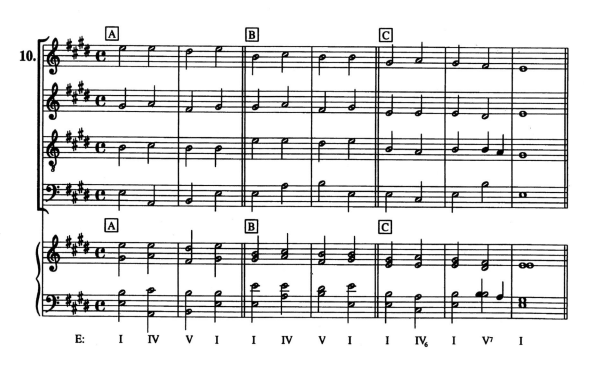

E: I IV V I I IV V I I IV₆ I V⁷ I

11.

Exercises 12 – 17   Keys of A and A♭ Major

A Major: the key name and tonic pitch are the note name above the last sharp (G♯)

do	re	mi	fa	sol	la	ti	do
1	2	3	4	5	6	7	1

12.

13.

14.

24

Ab Major: the key name and tonic pitch are the name of the next to the last flat (Ab)

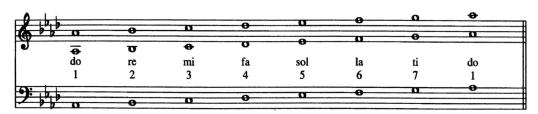

do	re	mi	fa	sol	la	ti	do
1	2	3	4	5	6	7	1

15.

16.

B533

26

<u>Exercises 18 – 26</u>   Eighth Rests

The example illustrates the counting of eighth rests.

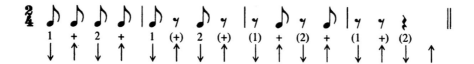

When first reading these exercises whisper the appropriate number or syllable on the rests, or sound "sh" for the duration of the rest. Remember to maintain a strong sense of downbeat-upbeat movement as you practice.

UNIT III

The Half Note as the Beat Unit

The half note as the beat unit introduces the concept of halving the rhythmic values of familiar notes. Four new meter signatures—$\frac{2}{2}$, ¢, $\frac{3}{2}$, and $\frac{4}{2}$ — and two new notes —the dotted whole note and the double whole note—are presented.

The chart compares notes written in $\frac{4}{4}$ and $\frac{4}{2}$ time.

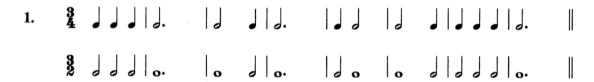

Exercises 1 – 5 $\frac{3}{2}$, $\frac{2}{2}$, and $\frac{4}{2}$ Meters
"Cut Time"—¢

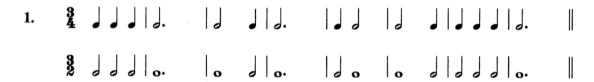

B533

Exercises 6 – 11   Melodies and Harmonizations in $\frac{3}{2}$, $\frac{4}{2}$, and $\frac{2}{2}$

Chant (count) the exercises on rhythmic syllables while tapping the beat. Then sing the melody/harmony while conducting the appropriate beat pattern.

8.

9.

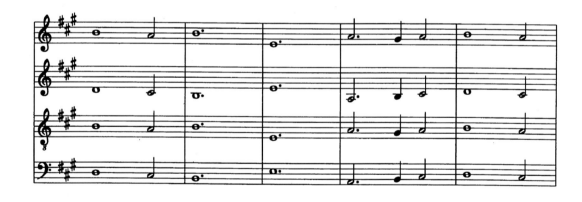

10.

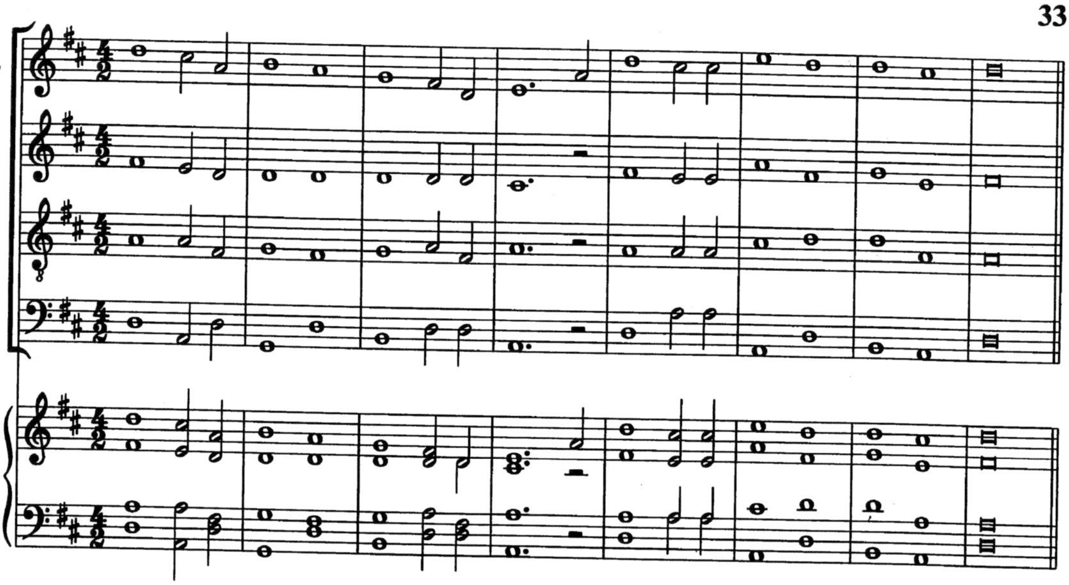

11.

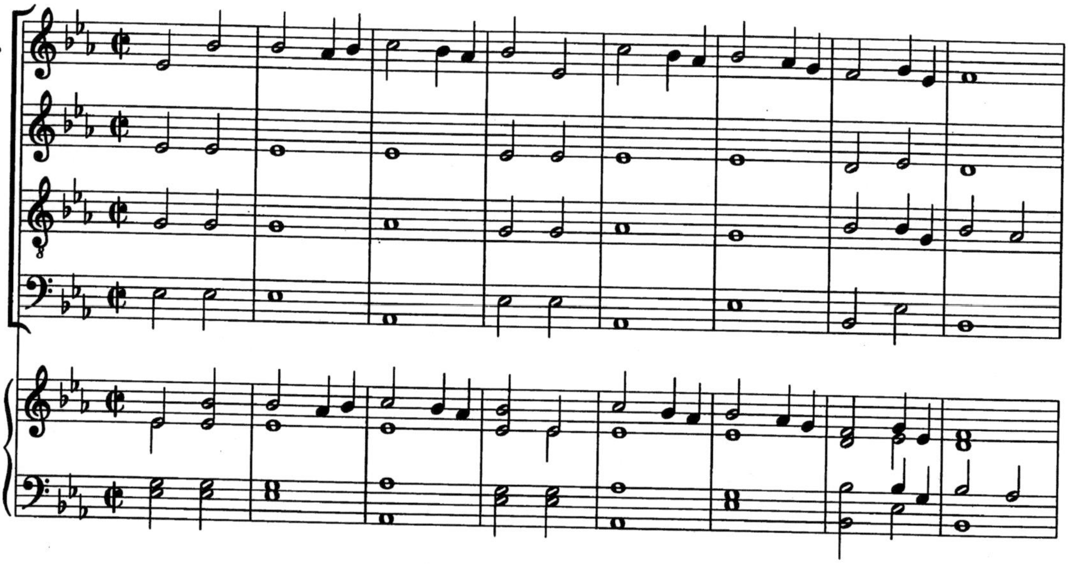

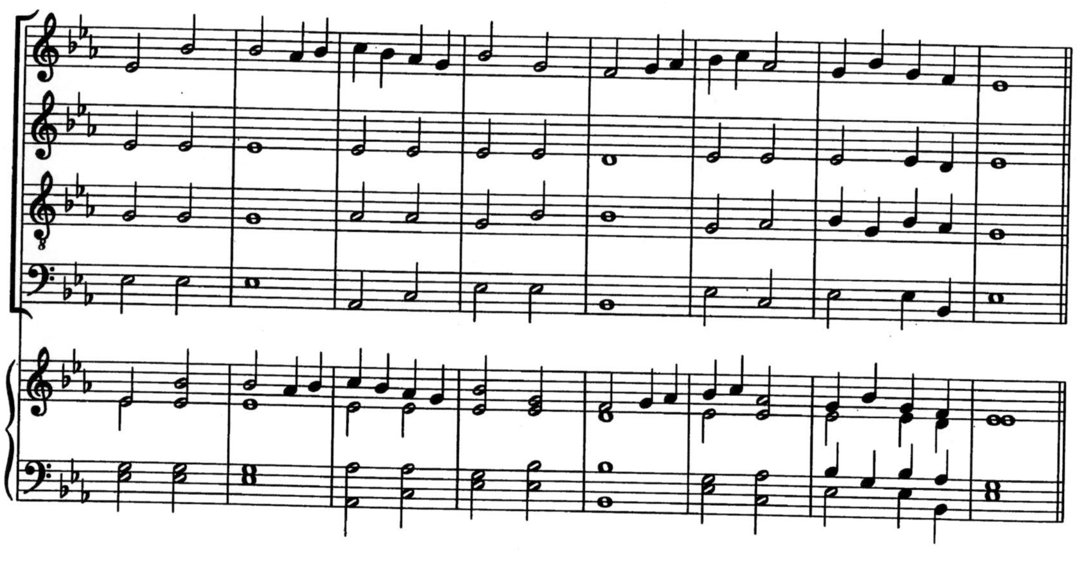

UNIT IV

Diatonic Interval Studies

The purpose of this unit is to:

1. train the eye to recognize intervals within a major scale
2. train the ear to hear those intervals
3. train the voice to correctly and comfortably negotiate them.

Before beginning practice on any exercise, set the tonality by singing the ascending and descending major scale.

Exercises 1 – 5   All Diatonic Intervals from the Tonic Pitch

1.

2.

Memorize and practice this exercise often.

Exercises 6 – 12   Major and Minor Thirds

8.

12.

Exercises 13 – 16   Perfect Fourths

13.

14.

UNIT V

The Triplet

This unit presents the triplet which divides the beat into three equal parts. The example illustrates one way of counting it.

Exercises 1 – 9   The Triplet
                     Duplets and Triplets

1.

2.

3.

4.

5.

6.

7.

8.

9.

Exercises 10 – 14   The Triplet Pattern —

10.

1 ta ta 2   1   ta 2   1 ta ta 2   ta 1 __

11.

14.

UNIT VI

Supertonic, Mediant, and Submediant Triads

<u>Exercises 1– 5</u>   Supertonic Triad—"re–fa–la–fa–re" or 2–4–6–4–2

1.

2.

D: I   ii   V⁷   I   I   ii   V⁷   I   I   ii   V   I

3.

Exercises 6 – 11   Mediant Triad—"mi–sol–ti–sol–mi" or 3–5–7–5–3

10.

11.

Exercises 12 – 15   Submediant Triad—"la–do–mi–do–la" or 6–1–3–1–6

12.

13.

14.

15.

Exercises 16 – 19   Four-part Practice using the
                     Supertonic, Mediant, and Submediant Triads

52

B533

UNIT VII

Easy Compound Time

The rhythmic principle implied in compound time is that the structural beat is represented by a dotted note which is divisible into three equal parts:

$$\text{♩.} \quad (\text{♪♪♪})$$

Compound Meters

The upper number is divided by 3 to arrive at the number of beats per measure

The <u>note value</u> indicated by the lower number (8) is multiplied by 3 to determine the type of note that receives 1 beat

6	divided by 3	= **2**
8	♪ multiplied by 3	= ♩.
9	divided by 3	= **3**
8	♪ multiplied by 3	= ♩.

Compare "like" notes and patterns in **2/4** and **6/8** time

Counting the rhythm

Exercises 1 – 9   Easy Patterns in 6/8 and 9/8 time

1.
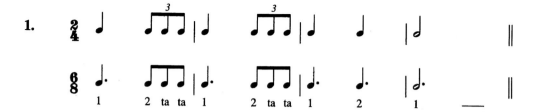

2.

3.

4.

5.

6.

B533

7.

8.

9.

<u>Exercises 10 – 12</u>   New patterns in Compound Time

10.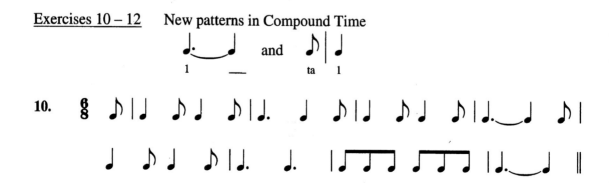

Exercises 13 – 18   The Pattern ♪ ♩   in 6/8 and 9/8

13.

14.

15. A. ...

B. ...

C. ...

D. ...

16. ...

UNIT VIII

Keys of C♭, C♯, F♯, G♭, D♭, and B Major

This unit introduces six new major keys. They will, however, seem somewhat familiar since, *with the exception of the key signature,* C♭ and C♯ look like C major on the staff. Likewise, F♯ = F; G♭ = G; D♭ = D; and B = B♭ major.

Since it is important for singers to develop a vocal sensation or "feel" of a note with its actual pitch, focus on this as you practice the exercises in this unit. (For instance, the key of F♯ major feels quite different vocally from the key of F major.)

Exercises 1 – 4   The Key of C♭ Major

Exercises 5 – 8   The Key of C♯ Major

Exercises 9 – 11   The Key of F# Major

9.

Exercises 12 – 14   The Key of Gb Major

After reading this exercise, compare it with #10 which is in the *enharmonic* key of F♯ major. Both exercises will sound the same even though they look very different on the page.

Exercises 15 – 19   The Key of D♭ Major

After mastering this exercise, review #7 which is its *enharmonic* equivalent.

B533

Exercises 20 – 24   The Key of B Major

Compare these chord progressions with Exercise 3 and note that they are aurally identical, even though #3 is written in 6/8 meter and in the key of C♭ major.

22.

24.

UNIT IX

The Eighth Note as the Beat Unit

The eighth note as the beat unit involves the concept of doubling the rhythmic value of familiar notes (those learned with the quarter note representing the beat). Three new meters—$\frac{2}{8}$, $\frac{3}{8}$, and $\frac{4}{8}$ are introduced in this unit.

The chart compares "like" notes in $\frac{4}{4}$ and $\frac{4}{8}$ meters.

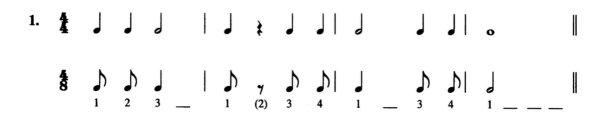

Exercises 1 – 6 $\frac{4}{8}$, $\frac{3}{8}$, and $\frac{2}{8}$ Meters

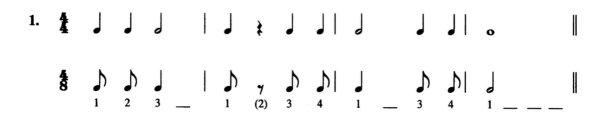

4.

5.

6.

<u>Exercises 7 – 10</u>   Sixteenth Notes in 3/8

7.

1 2 + 3   1 _ 3   1 + 2 + 3   1 _ _ 1 _ 3   1 + 2 3   1 _ _ 1 (2) (3)

8.

9.

B533

10.

Exercises 11 – 13   A New Rhythmic Pattern—♪. ♪ or ♩.♪

11.

Exercises 14 – 15   Two New Patterns— ♪ ♩   ♪ and ♪ ♩.

UNIT X

Natural and Harmonic Minor Keys

Minor tonality is presented in this unit using the "la minor" system of reading. Therefore, the first note of the minor scale will be called "la" (or 6), and the tonic triad will be labeled "la-do-mi-do-la" (or 6-1-3-1-6).

Movable syllables and numbers for natural minor keys.

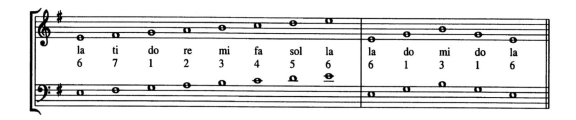

| la | ti | do | re | mi | fa | sol | la | la | do | mi | do | la |
| 6 | 7 | 1 | 2 | 3 | 4 | 5 | 6 | 6 | 1 | 3 | 1 | 6 |

Exercises 1 – 8   Major Keys Introduce Natural Minor Keys

1.

2.

3.

B533

Exercises 9 – 17   Natural Minor Keys
                           Skips in the Tonic, Subdominant, and Dominant Triads in Minor

The harmonic form of the minor scale uses an altered pitch—the raised seventh scale degree, which functions as a leading tone. In the "la minor" system, this note is called "si". (When using the movable number system, it is called "ti".)

Harmonic minor scale.

Exercises 18 – 21   Major Keys Introduce Harmonic Minor Keys

Exercises 22 – 29   Harmonic Minor Keys

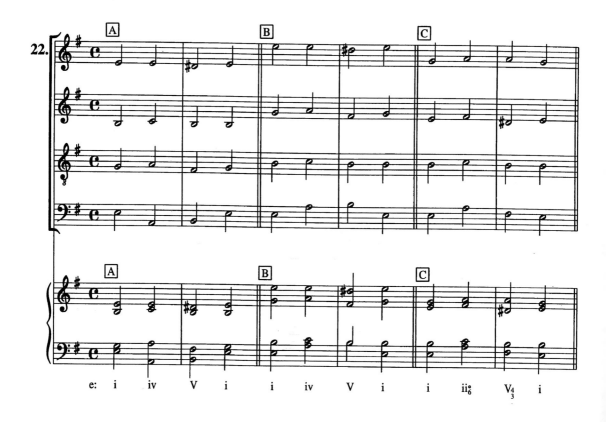

e: i   iv   V   i   i   iv   V   i   i   ii°$_6$ V$_3^4$ i

88

B533

Exercises 30 – 31   Modulation

UNIT XI

The Raised Fourth Scale Degree—"Fi"

The raised fourth scale degree, "fi", usually functions in one of three ways:

1. as an altered pitch in a melodic line
2. as a member of an altered chord
3. as the means for modulation to a new key (the dominant)

If you know hand signs for solfege syllables, be sure to use them as you practice these exercises.

Exercises 1 – 4   "Fi" used as an Altered Tone

92

Exercises 5 – 7   "Fi" used in Altered Chords

94

7.

B533

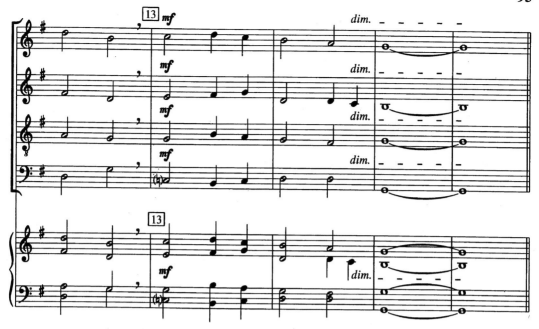

Exercises 8 – 11   "Fi" used in New Melodic Patterns

98

Songs for Sight-Singing

VOLUME 1

High School-SATB (B372)
High School-Treble (B370)
High School-Tenor/Bass (B371)
High School-Junior High School SAB (B376)
Junior High School-SATB (B375)
Junior High School-Treble (B373)
Junior High School-Tenor/Bass (B374)

VOLUME 2

High School-SATB (B516)
High School-Treble (B514)
High School-Tenor/Bass (B515)
High School/Junior High School SAB (B520)
Junior High School-SATB (B519)
Junior High School-Treble (B517)
Junior High School-Tenor/Bass (B518)

Southern
MUSIC
Exclusively Distributed By
HAL•LEONARD
CORPORATION
sales@halleonard.com